STOP HARMING ANIMALS!!!

By

@FrenteCívico

Chapter 1: In the Shadow of History: Humans and Animals Through Time

In the silent dawns of prehistory, beneath the sprawling canopies of ancient forests and across the vast, unyielding savannas, the fate of humanity was inseparably intertwined with the animal kingdom. This bond, formed in the crucible of survival, has been a constant driver of evolution, culture, and morality. Through the ages, as civilizations rose and fell, the story of human-animal relationships has been written with both tenderness and brutality, demonstrating our capacity for compassion and our penchant for dominance.

The early chapters of human history are replete with tales of animals regarded as deities, embodying strength, wisdom, or fertility in myriad cultures. They were the companions of deities, symbols of celestial power, and guides for the departed souls journeying into the afterlife. Simultaneously, the domestication of animals heralded the dawn of agriculture and settled life, forever altering the landscape of human society. This pivotal transition saw animals becoming integral to human survival, not just as companions but as sources of food, labor, and clothing. This duality of reverence and utilitarianism has pervaded our historical narrative, revealing a complex relationship fraught with contradiction yet rich in mutual benefit.

As centuries turned, industrial advances brought forth new challenges and opportunities. The Industrial Revolution, while a leap forward for human society, marked the beginning of an era of profound exploitation of both animal and environmental resources. The advancement of human civilization came at a steep cost: the ecosystems that sustain life and the countless animals caught in the crosshairs of progress. This period underscored a growing disconnect between humanity and the natural world, a rift that would only widen with the advent of modernity.

Yet, as the shadow of exploitation grew, so too did the light of awareness and compassion. The 20th century witnessed the burgeoning of a movement that would challenge the status quo and advocate for a radical rethinking of our relationship with animals. Inspired by the recognition of animals as sentient beings capable of suffering and joy, animal liberation movements emerged as a force for change. Organizations like PETA and countless others across the globe have since spearheaded efforts to ensure the rights and welfare of animals, promoting a vision of coexistence rooted in respect and empathy.

This transformative period has also illuminated the intricate connections between animal welfare and the health of our planet. The devastating impacts of unchecked animal agriculture, deforestation, and pollution have revealed an undeniable truth: the liberation of animals from cruelty and exploitation goes hand in hand with the stewardship of Earth's ecosystems. As our understanding of these connections deepens, the call to action becomes clear, urging a collective shift towards compassionate choices and sustainable living.

This book thus, is not just a reflection on the past; it is a clarion call for the future. It asks us to look back at our shared history with animals, not to dwell in the shadows of regret but to find the light of understanding and compassion. As we turn the pages of this chapter, we are invited to reevaluate our ethical stances, to recognize the intrinsic value of all living beings, and to embrace a path forward that honors our interconnectedness with the animal kingdom and the natural world.

The call of animal liberation is, at its heart, a call for humanity to return to a state of balance and empathy, to reforge a world where every being is respected, and no creature is left in harm's way. This journey, undertaken together, promises not just the salvation of our fellow beings but the rediscovery of our own humanity, nestled in the shadow of history, reaching out towards the light of a compassionate future.

Chapter 2: The Urgency of Change: Reassessing Our Relationship with Animals

As we stand at the crossroads of history and destiny, the echoes of our ancestors' footsteps still resonate beneath the canopy of modern civilization. But the path ahead beckons with a challenge unparalleled in our shared journey: to fundamentally reassess and transform our relationship with the myriad forms of life that share this planet with us. This chapter explores the urgent necessity of this transformation, considering the welfare of animals and the health of our environment as inseparable from our own future.

Reflecting on Past Inertia

Our history is steeped in a tradition where animals were viewed more as resources than beings capable of feeling. Centuries of inertia have rooted us in practices and beliefs that justify their exploitation under the guise of cultural norms and economic imperatives. This inertia is not just a static force; it is a dynamic part of our interactions with the animal world, shaping everything from dietary choices to fashion, entertainment, and labor. A critical reflection on this past is imperative, not to assign blame but to understand the depth of change required. We must ask ourselves how the traditions that once served us might now be hindering our ethical progress.

The Call for Ethical Reassessment

The evolving tapestry of human society, with its advances in understanding and empathy, demands that we reassess our ethical frameworks concerning animal rights. The notion that animals exist solely for human use is an archaic concept that fails to align with our growing recognition of their sentient nature. Ethical reassessment begins with acknowledging the intrinsic value of all life forms and considering the impact of our choices on their well-being. A shift in perspective is required—a move from seeing animals as commodities to recognizing them as fellow beings deserving of respect, dignity, and compassion.

Bridging Compassion and Rights Protection

The philosophy of animal liberation serves as a crucial bridge between compassion for other beings and the protection of their rights. It challenges us to reimagine our relationship with animals, advocating for a transition from exploitation to coexistence. This reimagined relationship does not merely end at stopping harm but extends to actively promoting well-being, ensuring that animals are not only free from pain and suffering but also live in environments that allow them to express their natural behaviors and social structures.

The inertia of our past attitudes carries with it not just ethical consequences but environmental ones as well. The pervasive impact of animal agriculture on deforestation, climate change, and biodiversity loss underscores the environmental imperative for change. Our inaction in the face of these implications represents a threat not only to countless species but to the very ecosystems that sustain human life. Addressing the environmental crisis demands a holistic approach, recognizing the role of animal welfare in the broader context of sustainability.

Advocating for Transformation

Understanding the urgency of change propels us toward advocacy for transformation. This advocacy is not a passive wish for a better world but an active effort to reshape our personal choices, societal structures, and global policies. It requires courage to confront uncomfortable truths, resilience to challenge entrenched norms, and imagination to envisage and forge a more compassionate, sustainable future.

Chapter 2 presents the irrefutable interconnectedness of all life, compelling a consensus that the time for change is not tomorrow, but today. The narrative woven here is one of hope and action, urging each of us to shoulder the mantle of ethical responsibility, environmental stewardship, and collective transformation. As we turn the page, let us carry forward the imperative to not only advocate for animal liberation but to embody the principles of compassion and sustainability in our daily lives, setting the stage for a profound and lasting change.

Chapter 3: The Call for Liberation: Advocacy for Animal Rights

Introduction

In the crucible of modern advocacy for animal rights, few organizations have stirred as much attention, controversy, and dialogue as PETA (People for the Ethical Treatment of Animals). With its uncompromising stance, eye-opening campaigns, and tireless activism, PETA has become synonymous with the fight against animal cruelty and exploitation. This chapter explores the journey of PETA, from its inception to its status today as a vanguard of the animal liberation movement, highlighting its indelible impact on the course of animal rights advocacy.

Origins and Evolution of PETA

Founded in 1980, PETA embarked on its mission with a simple yet profound principle: animals are not ours to experiment on, eat, wear, use for entertainment, or exploit in any other way. The organization's genesis was marked by a groundbreaking investigation into the mistreatment of monkeys in a laboratory in Silver Spring, Maryland, setting the tone for its future endeavors. Over decades, PETA has expanded its reach globally, utilizing high-profile campaigns, undercover investigations, and legal actions to challenge and change the ways in which societies view and treat animals. Each milestone in PETA's history reflects a larger narrative of evolving social consciousness and the growing imperative for ethical treatment of all sentient beings.

Towards a Paradigm Shift in Animal Advocacy

PETA's advocacy eschews incrementalism, aiming instead for a paradigm shift in the perception and treatment of animals. Through provocative campaigns and partnerships with celebrities, PETA has brought animal rights into mainstream discourse, challenging societal norms and sparking debates on issues ranging from fur farming to animal testing. Its approach—characterized by a blend of shock, compassion, and undeniable facts—has not only raised awareness but also fostered significant changes, including the adoption of cruelty-free practices by cosmetics companies and the closure of exploitative animal shows and circuses.

The Intersection of Ethics and Action

At the heart of PETA's mission lies a deep ethical commitment to animal liberation. Drawing from philosophical underpinnings that recognize the inherent value and rights of all sentient beings, PETA's actions strive to align human practices with these ethical imperatives. Whether through litigation to protect the rights of animals or the promotion of veganism as a means to end animal suffering, PETA exemplifies how ethics can guide impactful action. This section delves into how PETA navigates the complex interplay of moral philosophy and pragmatism, working to transform ethical considerations into concrete outcomes for animals.

Amplifying Voices for Change

PETA's ability to galvanize support and catalyze grassroots movements underscores the power of collective action. By amplifying the voices of those who advocate for animal rights and mobilizing a global community, PETA has succeeded in challenging entrenched interests and sparking legislative and corporate policy reforms. Through a combination of education, advocacy, and direct action, PETA encourages individuals and communities to become active participants in the movement for animal liberation, demonstrating how widespread change can arise from shared commitment and action.

Paving the Way for Environmental Consciousness

PETA's work also illuminates the inextricable link between animal liberation and environmental sustainability. By advocating for plant-based diets and challenging destructive agricultural practices, PETA not only fights for animal rights but also promotes a more sustainable and compassionate world for future generations. This section highlights how PETA's campaigns against factory farming and habitat destruction contribute to broader environmental conservation efforts, showcasing the organization's role in fostering a holistic ethical approach that encompasses both animal welfare and ecological health.

Through its relentless pursuit of animal liberation, PETA has not only reshaped the landscape of animal rights advocacy but also challenged individuals and societies to reconsider their relationships with the non-human inhabitants of our planet. As we reflect on PETA's journey and its contributions to the cause of compassion and justice, we are reminded of the ongoing struggles against cruelty and the collective power of advocacy to forge a more ethical, sustainable world. Chapter 3, in capturing the spirit and achievements of PETA, sets the stage for deeper exploration into the ways we can all contribute to the monumental task of ensuring rights, respect, and liberation for all sentient beings, paving the way toward true environmental and ethical harmony.

Chapter 4: Ethical Progress: The Foundation of Animal Liberation

Throughout the annals of history, the intricate tapestry of human-animal relationships has woven a narrative of companionship, exploitation, and evolution. As we cast our gaze back into the shadows of time, we witness the ebb and flow of societal attitudes towards our fellow sentient beings. From the shadows of our shared past emerges a profound realization: the treatment of animals serves as a barometer of our ethical progress as a society, laying a fundamental groundwork for the principles underpinning the concept of animal liberation.

Today, the clarion call for change reverberates with a sense of urgency as we stand at a crossroads, compelled to reassess and reconfigure our relationship with animals in the modern world. Long-held notions of dominance and subjugation are giving way to a burgeoning movement for liberation, spearheaded by influential organizations like PETA and a wave of impassioned advocates championing the cause of animal rights. This seismic shift urges us to interrogate our values, scrutinize our actions, and catalyze a transformation towards a society founded on compassion, empathy, and the intrinsic moral worth of all sentient beings.

Through the lens of a compassionate perspective, the recognition of sentience extends beyond the confines of traditional pet companionship to encompass the oft-forgotten voices of animals in the agricultural realm, including the gentle cows, loyal dogs, and enigmatic cats that grace our lives. This paradigm shift challenges us to transcend the boundaries of exploitation, prompting a profound reconsideration of our interactions with animals guided by a newfound ethos of respect, understanding, and ethical stewardship.

As we look at the intricate web of consequences wrought by animal agriculture on our environment, the stark realities of greenhouse gas emissions, climate change impacts, habitat degradation, and loss of biodiversity come sharply into focus. Illuminated by revelatory documentaries such as "Seaspiracy" and "Cowspiracy," our collective consciousness is awakened to the intricate interplay between our dietary choices and the environmental footprint we leave behind.

In the crucible of ethical and environmental consciousness, the advocacy for a paradigm shift gains momentum, heralding a clarion call for a moratorium on animal agriculture grounded in ethical imperatives and environmental exigencies. Embracing the transformative power of veganism and plant-based diets emerges as a tangible conduit towards reducing our ecological footprint and combating the pervasive tendrils of environmental degradation, inviting individuals to harmonize their values with their everyday choices in a bid to enact positive change for the planet we call home.

In the grand tapestry of our collective narrative, animal liberation emerges not merely as a philosophical concept but as a strategic imperative for environmental sustainability and ethical evolution. By forging robust connections between our treatment of animals and the intricate web of life that sustains us, we embark on a journey towards a compassionate future where collective action, mindful choices, and ethical fortitude converge to forge a path of healing for our planet and a legacy of harmony with all sentient beings.

Chapter 5: Compassion for all Sentient Beings: A Moral Obligation

Within the intricate tapestry of ethical discourse, the radiant thread of compassion for all sentient beings emerges as a luminous cornerstone, illuminating the moral landscape with its profound significance. Beyond a mere virtue to be admired, compassion unfolds as an intrinsic and binding moral obligation, transcending the boundaries of species and self-interest to embrace a universal ethos of empathy and respect. As we embark on a profound exploration of animal liberation and the confluence of ethics and empathy, we are beckoned to delve deep into the wellspring of compassion, recognizing it not just as a choice, but as an immutable duty inherent to our shared humanity and stewardship of the Earth.

At the heart of compassion lies the transformative power of empathy - the ability to see ourselves reflected in the eyes of other sentient beings, to acknowledge their inherent worth, and to extend a hand of kindness and care across species lines. It is a call to transcend the barriers of difference and embrace a holistic perspective that reveres the sanctity of life in all its forms. This expansive vision of compassion urges us to honor the interconnectedness of all living beings, weaving a narrative of unity and kinship that transcends physical boundaries and speaks to the profound interconnectedness of all life.

Embracing our moral obligation towards all sentient beings requires a profound recognition of their capacity for joy, pain, and suffering - emotions that resonate universally across the spectrum of existence. To turn a blind eye to the plight of our fellow creatures is to betray the very essence of our humanity and forsake the sacred bond that unites us in our shared journey on this planet. It is within this crucible of shared sentience and vulnerability that the moral imperative of compassion is forged, compelling us to extend our circle of ethical concern, advocacy, and solidarity to encompass the voices of the voiceless and the plight of the vulnerable.

As we navigate the complex terrain of ethical deliberations and moral quandaries, the cultivation of compassion transcends individual acts of kindness to evolve into a collective commitment to systemic change and social transformation. It becomes a unifying force that galvanizes communities, institutions, and nations to stand in solidarity with the marginalized, to challenge structures of oppression and exploitation, and to forge a path towards a world where compassion flows as an eternal river, nourishing the roots of justice, equity, and respect for all living beings.

In essence, the journey towards animal liberation finds its moral compass in the unwavering mandate to extend compassion to all sentient beings, recognizing their intrinsic dignity and right to live free from harm and suffering. It calls upon us to internalize the universal truth of interconnectedness, empathy, and ethical responsibility, weaving a tapestry of compassion that illuminates the path towards a harmonious coexistence where all beings - human, animal, and environmental - thrive in a symphony of unity and reverence for life. Through the luminous prism of compassion, we discover not just a moral obligation, but a sacred covenant to honor the sanctity of all sentient beings and to forge a future where the chorus of empathy resounds louder than the cacophony of indifference, and the light of compassion guides our collective journey towards a world where love, respect, and kinship reign supreme.

Chapter 6: Dogs, Cats, and More: Acknowledging Sentience Across Species

Introduction

In embarking upon a journey through the landscapes of sentience that dogs, cats, and cows inhabit, Chapter 6 offers a deep dive into the core of what makes these beings not merely alive but vividly sentient. It is not just an exploration but an invitation to reconsider the ethical grounds on which we base our interactions with them. Recognizing the capacity for suffering and joy across species challenges us to confront the moral implications of our choices and actions towards these animals, who share more with us than meets the eye.

The Depths of Sentience

Sentience—the capacity to feel pain and pleasure—serves as the cornerstone of our ethical obligations towards other beings. This section unfolds the complex tapestry of emotional and cognitive capacities that define the sentient experience, bridging the gap between humans and animals. By examining the scientific evidence and philosophical arguments for animal sentience, this segment encourages a profound reassessment of how we view animals, urging a shift from seeing them as objects of use to recognizing them as subjects of a life filled with their own experiences and desires.

Canine Companions: The Bonds of Empathy

Dogs, with their unparalleled loyalty and emotional availability, have carved a special place in human society and our hearts. This section explores the deep empathy that characterizes the human-dog relationship, reflecting on how our canine companions teach us about unconditional love, loyalty, and the joy of living in the moment. However, it also calls for a reciprocal understanding and compassion towards dogs, emphasizing the importance of respecting their needs, personalities, and well-being, beyond the confines of human expectations and desires.

Feline Grace: Embracing Diverse Sentience

Cats, with their mysterious allure and independent spirit, offer a different lens through which to view sentience. This section delves into the enigmatic world of felines, celebrating their unique expressions of consciousness and individuality. By highlighting the sophisticated ways in which cats communicate, form bonds, and navigate their environments, this segment argues for a greater appreciation and respect for the subjective experiences of cats, advocating for their right to live lives free from undue human imposition and harm.

Bovine Majesty: Rethinking Our Relationship with Cows

Cows, often relegated to the status of agricultural commodities, are revealed in this section as creatures of profound emotional depth and social complexity. Through insights into their social bonds, communicative expressions, and emotional responses, this segment challenges prevailing norms of exploitation and indifference. It calls for a radical reevaluation of our relationship with cows and all farmed animals — urging a shift towards practices that honor their dignity, cater to their natural behaviors, and acknowledge their right to a life free from suffering.

A Spectrum of Sentience: Bridging Understanding Across Species

This pivotal section weaves together the threads of sentience across our canine, feline, and bovine brethren, emphasizing the rich tapestry of life that connects humans with other animals. By drawing parallels in the capacity for emotion, social connection, and enjoyment of life across species, it highlights the moral imperatives that arise from this shared sentience. The chapter calls on us to broaden our circle of compassion, urging a universal acknowledgment of the rights and value of every sentient being, irrespective of species.

This section should serves as a poignant reflection on the shared journey of life that connects humans with animals — indeed, with all sentient beings. It underscores the profound ethical obligation we bear to extend our compassion, empathy, and respect to every creature capable of experiencing joy and suffering. In recognizing the intrinsic value and sentience that transcend species boundaries, we are called upon to advocate for a world where all beings are afforded the dignity and rights they rightfully deserve. This chapter not only enlightens but also inspires a rekindled commitment to a more compassionate, equitable coexistence with the non-human animals with whom we share our world.

Chapter 7: Conservation Ethics and Biodiversity Preservation

At the heart of the environmental movement lies a crucial intersection - that of conservation ethics and the urgent need to preserve biodiversity. This chapter delves deep into these intertwined principles, exploring both the ethical foundations and the pragmatic solutions critical for protecting the rich tapestry of life on Earth. Our journey through conservation ethics and biodiversity preservation illuminates the inherent value of life in all its diversity and the shared responsibility to safeguard our planet's ecological balance.

The Ethics of Biodiversity

Biodiversity, the variety and variability of life on Earth, is not just an asset but a testament to the complex beauty of our natural world. This section argues that the intrinsic value of diverse species and ecosystems warrants a moral imperative for preservation. Drawing from philosophies that place intrinsic worth on all forms of life, it explores how ethical frameworks guide our conservation efforts. Whether through the lens of deep ecology, which posits equal value on all living beings, or the biotic ethic that Aldo Leopold famously encapsulated as "thinking like a mountain," this discourse emphasizes a profound respect for the interconnectedness of life.

Balancing Human Needs and Conservation Goals

The crux of conservation lies not just in the protection of nature but in reconciling this goal with the needs of human populations. This section examines the delicate balance between human development and ecological preservation, advocating for sustainable practices that ensure the health of our planet while providing for human welfare. It unpacks ethical decision-making processes that enable societies to thrive without compromising the environment, highlighting the imperative for solutions that foster both environmental integrity and human well-being.

Threats to Biodiversity

The path to biodiversity preservation is fraught with obstacles - habitat destruction, climate change, pollution, and overexploitation, to name a few. This section not only casts a light on these pressing threats but also emphasizes our ethical responsibility to counteract them. It calls for a proactive stance, infused with stewardship and ecological mindfulness, to mitigate the impacts of our anthropogenic footprint. The essence of this discussion revolves around the moral imperative to leave behind a planet that future generations can cherish and thrive in.

Conservation Strategies and Initiatives

Within the field of biodiversity conservation, there are beacons of hope. This section showcases a range of successful conservation strategies and initiatives from around the globe, from community-based conservation efforts that empower local populations to international agreements that protect critical habitats. It highlights how innovative approaches, such as protected area management and species recovery programs, are making strides in preserving the rich diversity of life. The stories and strategies discussed exemplify collaborative efforts, illustrating how collective action can lead to meaningful environmental restoration and protection.

The Role of Ethics in Environmental Decision-Making

As the chapter approaches its conclusion, the focus shifts to the critical role ethics plays in environmental decision-making. Ethical considerations act as a compass guiding the complex process of balancing ecological integrity with human aspirations. This section stresses the importance of ethical leadership and ecological literacy in shaping policies and practices. It underlines a commitment to future generations, advocating for decision-making processes that are informed by a deep-seated moral obligation to the natural world.

In summary, this work reiterates the indispensable role of conservation ethics in navigating the relationship between humanity and the earth. It calls for a renewed and collective commitment to preserving biodiversity, not merely as a duty but as a moral imperative. By fostering ethical stewardship and adopting sustainable practices, we embark on a path toward a flourishing world, honoring the complex web of life that sustains us all. This chapter serves as a clarion call to action, urging us to embrace our role as guardians of the planet's extraordinary biodiversity.

Chapter 8: Sustainable Agriculture and Ethical Food Practices—A Path Towards Animal Liberation

We must reimage the essence of sustainable agriculture and ethical food practices through the lens of animal liberation. Confront the current paradigms of food production that compromise animal welfare and environmental health, advocating for a transformative approach that centers on compassion, ecological harmony, and ethical integrity. This chapter argues for the development of food systems that not only ensure human well-being but also fundamentally respect the intrinsic value of all living beings.

Foundations of Compassionate Agriculture

At the heart of sustainable agriculture lies the potential for a radical shift towards practices that recognize the rights and welfare of animals. This section lays the groundwork for such a transformation, detailing methods of agricultural production that align with the principles of animal liberation. It explores alternative farming systems, like agroecology and permaculture, which integrate plant-based food production and support natural ecosystems without relying on animal exploitation. The focus is on creating a food system that is not only sustainable but inherently compassionate, highlighting the ethical obligation to cease the commodification of animal life for agricultural purposes.

Ethical Considerations in Food Production

The ethics of food production are scrutinized with an emphasis on animal rights. This section challenges conventional agricultural practices that treat animals as mere production units, subjecting them to cruelty and deprivation. It delves into the moral imperatives of recognizing animals as sentient beings with inherent rights, advocating for a shift towards plant-based diets as a cornerstone of ethical food practices. By examining the ethical dilemmas inherent in animal farming, including confinement, separation of families, and premature death, the narrative underscores the urgent need for a paradigm shift towards food systems that honor the dignity and life of every being.

Championing Plant-Based Nutrition for All

To address the dual objectives of human nutrition and animal liberation, this section advocates for a global transition towards plant-based diets. It emphasizes the nutritional adequacy and health benefits of plant-based foods, debunking myths around protein deficiency and highlighting the abundance of nutrients provided by a diverse, vegan diet. Moreover, it explores how plant-based food systems can promote food sovereignty, reduce world hunger, and ensure equitable access to nutritious foods, thereby aligning ethical food practices with broader social and environmental justice goals.

Ending Food Waste and Reducing Environmental Harm

Adopting sustainable, plant-based food systems also offers a viable solution to reducing food waste and mitigating environmental damage. This section examines the disproportionate use of resources in animal agriculture—land, water, and energy—and its role in exacerbating food waste and environmental degradation. By transitioning to plant-based agriculture, we can drastically cut down on the ecological footprint of food production, preserving vital resources and protecting biodiversity. This part of the narrative not only calls for an end to wasteful practices but also for a collective, ethical responsibility towards minimizing our impact on the planet.

We propose a vision for a future where sustainable agriculture and ethical food practices work hand in hand with the principles of animal liberation. It calls for a profound reevaluation of our food systems, urging a shift away from exploitative practices towards a model that respects the sanctity of all life. As the chapter concludes, it implores readers to consider their role in fostering change, advocating for choices that reflect compassion, sustainability, and justice. By embracing the ethos of animal liberation within our food systems, we pave the way for a more ethical, equitable, and thriving world for all living beings.

Chapter 10: Embracing Animal Liberation through Sustainable Living and Ethical Economics

In Chapter 10, we embark on a transformative journey that intertwines the principles of sustainable living and ethical consumerism with a steadfast commitment to animal liberation. This chapter illuminates how individual choices, values, and consumption patterns can engender a more compassionate, sustainable world that respects and upholds the rights of all living beings. By advocating for the harmonious coexistence of humans and animals within the framework of eco-conscious practices, we strive towards a future where ethical considerations permeate every facet of daily life.

The Foundations of Compassionate Living

Sustainable living finds its true essence in a lifestyle rooted in compassion and respect for all creatures. This section articulates the foundational principles of living in harmony with animals, emphasizing the reduction of waste, the conservation of resources, and the promotion of ethical consumer habits that reject products derived from animal exploitation. It underscores the crucial role of individual agency in fostering sustainable choices that prioritize the well-being of our planet and its diverse inhabitants, both human and non-human.

Advocating Ethical Consumerism for Animal Welfare

Ethical consumerism takes center stage as a potent tool for advancing animal liberation and environmental stewardship. This section delves into the impact of conscious consumer decisions on animal welfare, sustainability, and ethical production standards. By encouraging informed and deliberate purchasing choices that reject products derived from animal suffering, consumers wield immense power in shaping demand-driven changes that promote transparency and ethical sourcing practices across supply chains.

Implementing Sustainable Habits in Daily Life

Practical sustainability unfolds as a transformative force in the everyday lives of individuals committed to animal liberation. This section offers practical guidance on integrating sustainable practices into daily routines, spanning from reducing reliance on single-use plastics and embracing renewable energy sources to supporting local, cruelty-free businesses and adopting eco-conscious modes of transportation. It advocates for a holistic approach to sustainable living that nurtures personal well-being while fostering a deep sense of accountability towards the welfare of animals and the environment.

Cultivating a Reverence for Nature and Animal Life

Amidst the bustling rhythms of modern living, reconnecting with nature and embracing a profound sense of ecological awareness becomes paramount for advancing animal liberation. This section emphasizes the intrinsic link between environmental stewardship and sustainable living, urging individuals to cultivate a deep appreciation for the beauty and interconnectedness of the natural world. By fostering sustainable lifestyle habits that honor and protect the Earth's ecosystems, we foster a culture of respect and compassion towards all living beings, nurturing a more harmonious coexistence between humans and animals.

Fostering Resilience, Well-Being, and Ethical Values

Chapter 10 culminates in a reflection on the symbiotic relationship between sustainable living practices, personal well-being, community resilience, and ethical values. It advocates for a holistic approach to sustainability that prioritizes health, happiness, and social connections while aligning with the core principles of ethical responsibility and environmental consciousness. By nurturing a lifestyle defined by ethical consumerism, sustainable choices, and a deep respect for all life forms, individuals pave the way for a more compassionate, equitable future for both present and future generations.

As we draws the section to a close, we make a call to action for collective engagement and individual mindfulness in embracing animal liberation through sustainable living practices and ethical consumerism. The narrative celebrates the transformative power of conscious choices, ethical values, and sustainable habits in fostering a world where compassion, sustainability, and respect for all living beings thrive. By embodying these principles in our daily lives, we chart a course towards a future where ethical considerations shape our interactions with the planet, its creatures, and each other, paving the way for a more just and harmonious world.

Chapter 11: Championing Animal Liberation within Environmental Justice and Social Equity

We must embark on a powerful exploration of the interconnected realms of environmental justice and social equity, underscoring the critical need to advocate for the rights and welfare of animals within these spheres. This chapter sheds light on the intricate web of environmental challenges faced by marginalized communities and propounds inclusive solutions that prioritize the intersectionality of environmental health, human dignity, and animal liberation. By weaving the principles of animal rights into the fabric of environmental justice and social equity, we take a stance for a more compassionate, sustainable world that embraces all living creatures as stakeholders deserving of justice and respect.

Upholding Environmental Justice for Animals

Central to the discourse of environmental justice is the concept of extending justice to all beings, including animals. This section lays the groundwork for environmental justice by expanding the scope to encompass the protection and well-being of non-human animals. It highlights the imperative to address systemic disparities in animal welfare, conservation efforts, and the equitable distribution of resources among all species. By advocating for the inclusion of animal rights within the framework of environmental justice, we pave the way for a more holistic approach to sustainability that embraces the intrinsic worth of all life forms.

Environmental Bias and Animal Exploitation

Delving into the intersections of environmental justice and animal liberation, this section exposes the environmental bias and exploitation faced by non-human animals. It sheds light on how animal agriculture, habitat destruction, and pollution disproportionately impact vulnerable animal populations, often mirroring the injustices endured by marginalized human communities. By confronting the systemic issues of animal exploitation within the environmental discourse, the narrative calls for a reevaluation of human-animal relationships that are rooted in compassion, respect, and ethical stewardship.

Activism, Allyship, and Animal Rights

Through narratives of activism and allyship, this section amplifies the voices of advocates who champion animal liberation as a core tenet of environmental justice. It celebrates the resilience and agency of individuals and communities dedicated to uplifting the rights of animals, showcasing the power of grassroots activism in effecting meaningful change. By standing in solidarity with animal advocates, environmental justice advocates, and social equity proponents, we create a united front that transcends boundaries and champions the inherent value of all life.

Policy Frameworks for Animal Rights and Environmental Equity

Exploring the intersection of animal rights and environmental justice within policy frameworks, this section delves into the role of legislation, advocacy, and community engagement in promoting equitable solutions for animals and the environment. It discusses initiatives aimed at fostering a more inclusive and compassionate approach to governance that values animal welfare as a cornerstone of environmental equity. By advocating for legislative measures that safeguard animal rights within the environmental justice framework, we pave a path towards a more just and humane world for all beings.

The Essence of Animal Liberation

Chapter 11 culminates in a reflective dialogue on the intersectionality of animal liberation, acknowledging the multifaceted dimensions of identity and species that intersect within the realm of environmental justice. It advocates for an inclusive and intersectional approach that centers on the interconnectedness of all living beings, encompassing diverse identities, and experiences in the pursuit of justice and equity. By recognizing the intricate interplay between human, animal, and environmental concerns, we foster a more compassionate and holistic vision of sustainability that celebrates the inherent worth of all life forms.

Let environmental justice, social equity, and animal liberation coexist harmoniously within our collective consciousness. It underscores the urgency of integrating animal rights into the discourse of environmental justice, advocating for a paradigm shift towards a more compassionate and inclusive approach to sustainability. By championing the rights and welfare of animals within the framework of environmental justice and social equity, we forge a path towards a more equitable, just, and compassionate future for all inhabitants of our shared planet.

Critical aspects of climate change mitigation and adaptation strategies need the emphasizing of the important intersection with animal liberation. Let's face the challenges posed by a changing climate, the urgent need for action to reduce greenhouse gas emissions, and the significance of preparing for and adapting to the impacts of climate change while considering the welfare and rights of animals.

Understanding Climate Change and Animal Impacts

Climate change affects us as well as animals. There are very significant impacts on biodiversity, habitats, and wildlife populations. We emphasizes the imperative for immediate action to address climate change not only for the well-being of humans but also for the protection and liberation of animals.

Climate change is a global crisis that poses severe threats to ecosystems and biodiversity, leading to habitat destruction, species extinction, and disruptions in animal migration patterns. Human activities, such as deforestation, industrial agriculture, and pollution, have not only contributed to global warming but also exacerbated the suffering and exploitation of animals. Understanding the interconnectedness between climate change and animal welfare is crucial in developing holistic solutions for a sustainable future.

Mitigation Strategies for Animal Welfare

By exploring mitigation strategies, we must find the way to reduce greenhouse gas emissions and environmental degradation that harm animals, promoting ethical considerations and animal liberation principles in climate action. It emphasizes the importance of transitioning to sustainable practices that respect and protect animals' rights and well-being.

Mitigation strategies for animal welfare focus on reducing the negative impacts of human activities on animals and their habitats.

Transitioning to plant-based diets, promoting cruelty-free practices, and advocating for animal rights are crucial steps in mitigating climate change while upholding the principles of compassion and justice for all beings. Sustainable agriculture, land conservation, and wildlife protection efforts play a vital role in preserving biodiversity and ensuring the welfare of animals in the face of a changing climate. Integrating animal liberation principles into climate mitigation strategies fosters a more ethical and sustainable approach to addressing environmental challenges.

Adaptation Strategies with Animal Welfare in Mind

Focusing on adaptation, this section addresses how communities can prepare for and respond to the impacts of climate change while safeguarding the welfare and rights of animals. It emphasizes the need for resilience-building measures that prioritize coexistence and harmony between humans and animals in adapting to environmental changes.

Adaptation to climate change requires considering the unique vulnerabilities and needs of animals in developing resilience strategies. Implementing wildlife corridors, protecting natural habitats, and establishing conservation areas are essential in facilitating the adaptation of animal populations to changing environmental conditions. Incorporating animal welfare considerations into disaster preparedness plans, emergency response protocols, and ecosystem restoration efforts helps mitigate the suffering and displacement of wildlife in the face of climate-related disasters. Building a climate-resilient future that respects and ensures the liberation of animals is integral to fostering sustainable coexistence and harmony between humans and the natural world.

Technological Innovations for Animal-Friendly Solutions

By highlighting technological innovations and solutions that prioritize animal welfare, this section explores how advancements in clean energy, sustainable agriculture, and biodiversity conservation can contribute to climate change mitigation and adaptation efforts while promoting the liberation of animals. It underscores the importance of leveraging technology for ethical and sustainable climate action that benefits all living beings.

Technological innovations that prioritize animal welfare and environmental sustainability are key to addressing climate change while respecting the rights and well-being of animals. Clean energy technologies, such as solar power and wind energy, offer renewable alternatives to fossil fuels, reducing greenhouse gas emissions and minimizing environmental harm to wildlife. Sustainable agriculture practices, such as regenerative farming and agroecology, support biodiversity conservation, soil health, and ecosystem resilience, promoting ethical land use that benefits both humans and animals. Biodiversity conservation initiatives, including habitat restoration and species protection programs, help safeguard animal populations and ecosystems from the impacts of climate change, ensuring their freedom and survival in a rapidly changing world. Integrating animal-friendly solutions into technological innovations enhances the ethical dimension of climate change mitigation and adaptation efforts, fostering a more compassionate and sustainable future for all beings.

Policy and Governance for Animal Rights and Environmental Justice

This section delves into the role of policy frameworks, international agreements, and governance structures in promoting animal rights, environmental justice, and climate action. It discusses the significance of regulatory mechanisms, ethical considerations, and inclusive decision-making processes that prioritize the liberation and well-being of animals within the context of climate change adaptation and mitigation strategies.

Policy and governance frameworks that advocate for animal liberation and environmental justice are essential in advancing climate action that respects the rights and interests of all beings. Incorporating animal welfare principles into climate policies, environmental regulations, and conservation strategies ensures that animals are recognized as sentient beings deserving of protection and compassion. International agreements, such as the Paris Agreement, provide a platform for global cooperation on climate change mitigation and adaptation efforts that integrate ethical considerations and animal rights perspectives. Governance structures that prioritize inclusivity, transparency, and ethical decision-making facilitate the development of policies that promote sustainable coexistence between humans and animals, advancing environmental justice and biodiversity conservation. By aligning policy and governance mechanisms with animal liberation values, we can create a more equitable and sustainable future that upholds the rights and dignity of all living beings on Earth.

Towards a Compassionate and Sustainable Future

In concluding Chapter 12, the narrative underscores the urgency of addressing climate change through a lens of animal liberation and ethics. It highlights the interconnectedness between human actions, environmental degradation, and animal suffering, emphasizing the need for compassionate and inclusive approaches to climate change mitigation and adaptation. By prioritizing animal welfare, environmental justice, and ethical decision-making in our collective efforts to combat climate change, we can create a more compassionate, sustainable, and harmonious world for present and

future generations of humans and animals alike.

Chapter 13: Animal Liberation: Ethical Considerations

We now dive into the critical aspects of animal liberation, ethical considerations, and the interconnectedness between human actions and the welfare of all living beings. This chapter emphasizes the urgency of addressing animal rights and liberation within the broader context of environmental sustainability and compassion towards all sentient creatures.

Understanding Animal Liberation

All of us must consider the foundation of the concept of animal liberation, highlighting the intrinsic value of animals and the ethical imperative to respect their rights and well-being. It delves into the history of animal rights movements, the moral considerations surrounding animal exploitation, and the necessity of promoting compassion and justice for all species.

Ethical Frameworks and Animal Rights

By examining ethical frameworks and philosophical perspectives on animal rights, this section discusses the moral arguments for treating animals with respect, empathy, and equality. It explores utilitarian, deontological, and rights-based approaches to animal ethics, emphasizing the need for a paradigm shift towards recognizing animals as individuals with inherent rights and intrinsic value.

Environmental Impact and Animal Liberation

Focusing on the environmental impact of animal agriculture, wildlife exploitation, and habitat destruction, this section highlights the interconnectedness between human activities, animal suffering, and ecological degradation. It addresses the moral implications of practices such as factory farming, deforestation, and species extinction, underscoring the urgency of promoting sustainable and ethical alternatives that prioritize animal welfare and environmental stewardship.

Animal Welfare Legislation and Advocacy

By examining animal welfare legislation, regulatory frameworks, and advocacy efforts, this section explores the role of legal protections and grassroots movements in advancing animal liberation. It discusses the importance of promoting humane treatment, animal rights education, and policy reforms that safeguard the rights and dignity of animals in various contexts, including agriculture, entertainment, and research.

Intersectionality and Animal Liberation

This section delves into the intersectionality between animal liberation and social justice movements, highlighting the interconnected struggles for equality, justice, and liberation. It explores how issues of race, gender, class, and speciesism intersect within systems of oppression and discrimination, emphasizing the need for solidarity, inclusivity, and intersectional approaches to advocating for the rights of all marginalized communities, including animals.

Towards a Compassionate Future

In concluding Chapter 13, we underscore the importance of embracing a future rooted in compassion, empathy, and ethical consideration for all living beings. It emphasizes the moral imperative of promoting animal liberation, environmental sustainability, and ethical consciousness in shaping a more just and harmonious world. By recognizing the inherent rights and dignity of animals, advocating for their liberation, and fostering a culture of empathy and respect towards all species, we can cultivate a more compassionate and sustainable future for present and future generations of humans and animals alike.

Transitioning Away from Animal Agriculture Towards Sustainable and Ethical Food Systems

The need to transition away from animal agriculture due to its detrimental impact on the planet and the inherent cruelty involved in the industry is URGENT. We advocate for banning animal agriculture and replacing it with lab-made food and plant-based products to promote sustainability, ethical practices, and compassion towards animals.

Rethinking Agriculture for a Sustainable Future

This section delves into the environmental degradation and cruelty inflicted by animal agriculture, emphasizing the urgent need to ban this industry. It discusses the environmental consequences of animal farming, such as deforestation, greenhouse gas emissions, and water pollution, and highlights the ethical concerns surrounding the treatment of animals in intensive farming systems.

Embracing Lab-Made Food and Plant-Based Alternatives

By advocating for the replacement of animal agriculture with lab-made food and plant-based products, this section explores sustainable alternatives that can meet global food demand while prioritizing animal welfare and environmental conservation. It discusses the benefits of lab-grown meat, plant-based proteins, and cruelty-free food options in reducing the environmental footprint of food production and promoting ethical food choices.

Transitioning to Ethical and Equitable Food Systems

Focusing on transitioning to ethical and equitable food systems, this section discusses the importance of promoting transparency, fairness, and compassion in the food industry. It emphasizes the need to support initiatives that prioritize animal welfare, ensure fair treatment of food system workers, and guarantee access to healthy and sustainable food for all individuals.

Emphasizing Innovation and Technology in Food Production

By highlighting the role of innovation and technology in food production, this section explores advancements in food technology that support the transition away from animal agriculture. It discusses the potential for sustainable farming practices, vertical farming, and food-processing innovations to revolutionize the way we produce and consume food, promoting environmental sustainability and ethical food choices.

Advocating for Legal and Policy Changes

This section delves into the importance of advocating for legal and policy changes that support the shift away from animal agriculture. It discusses the need for government regulations, industry standards, and public initiatives that promote the ban on animal farming, incentivize the adoption of sustainable food practices, and ensure a smooth transition towards a more ethical and sustainable food system.

A Compassionate and Sustainable Food Future

Concluding here, we stress the imperative of transitioning away from animal agriculture towards sustainable and ethical food systems. By banning animal agriculture, embracing lab-made food and plant-based alternatives, and advocating for innovative and compassionate food practices, we can pave the way for a more sustainable, ethical, and compassionate future for animals, the planet, and all individuals involved in the food system.

In the context of emphasizing animal liberation and addressing the urgent need to combat climate change, it's crucial to recognize the interconnectedness of these two critical issues. Here are some key points to consider when discussing the intersection of animal liberation and climate change mitigation:

1. Reducing Carbon Footprint: The livestock industry, particularly industrial animal agriculture, is a significant contributor to greenhouse gas emissions, deforestation, and land degradation. By transitioning towards plant-based diets and reducing consumption of animal products, individuals can significantly decrease their carbon footprint and mitigate climate change.

2. Preserving Biodiversity: Protecting biodiversity is essential for maintaining resilient ecosystems that can adapt to climate change. Animal liberation includes advocating for the preservation of wildlife habitats, protecting endangered species, and promoting conservation efforts to safeguard biodiversity and ecosystem services vital for climate resilience.

3. **Promoting Sustainable Agriculture:** Supporting regenerative agriculture practices that prioritize soil health, biodiversity conservation, and carbon sequestration can help mitigate climate change impacts. By promoting agroecological farming methods and sustainable land use practices, we can reduce greenhouse gas emissions, enhance soil fertility, and promote food security without relying on industrial animal agriculture.

4. Raising Awareness: Educating the public about the environmental impacts of animal agriculture, deforestation for livestock grazing, and the connections between animal exploitation and climate change is crucial. By raising awareness about these interconnected issues, individuals can make informed choices that promote both animal welfare and climate resilience.

5. Advocating for Policy Change: Advocating for policies that support sustainable food systems, animal welfare regulations, and climate-friendly initiatives is essential. By engaging with policymakers, supporting legislative reforms, and promoting environmentally sustainable practices, we can address the root

causes of climate change and promote a more compassionate, sustainable future for all beings.

By integrating discussions on animal liberation, climate change mitigation, and environmental sustainability, we can cultivate a holistic approach to addressing the interconnected challenges facing our planet and create a more harmonious relationship with the natural world.

Water Conservation and Advocating for Ending Animal Agriculture

This chapter delves into the critical aspects of water resource management and conservation while shining a spotlight on the urgent need to end animal agriculture. It addresses the challenges posed by water scarcity, pollution, and unsustainable water use practices, emphasizing the impacts of animal agriculture on water resources and the environment.

Water Resources and Animal Agriculture

This section provides an overview of water resources, highlighting the significant water footprint of animal agriculture. It discusses how livestock production, feed crops, and intensive farming practices contribute to water scarcity, pollution, and environmental degradation.

Water Scarcity and the Role of Animal Agriculture

Examining water scarcity, this section explores how animal agriculture exacerbates water stress in regions globally. It delves into the implications of excessive water use in the meat and dairy industry, the strain on freshwater ecosystems, and the urgent need to address these challenges by transitioning away from animal agriculture.

Sustainable Water Management Practices and Plant-Based Solutions

Focusing on sustainable water management practices, this section advocates for transitioning to plant-based diets as a key strategy to reduce water consumption and promote water conservation. It discusses the potential of plant-based agriculture in alleviating water scarcity, mitigating pollution, and fostering sustainable water use practices.

Water Quality, Pollution Control, and Animal Agriculture

Addressing water quality and pollution control, this section examines how animal agriculture contributes to water pollution through runoff, waste disposal, and chemical usage. It explores the environmental implications of animal agriculture on water quality and the urgent need to adopt sustainable farming practices to protect water resources.

Climate Change, Water Adaptation, and Ending Animal Agriculture

By exploring climate change adaptation in water management, this section underscores the interconnected impacts of animal agriculture on climate change and water resources. It advocates for ending animal agriculture as a crucial step toward mitigating greenhouse gas emissions, preserving water resources, and building resilience in the face of climate change.

In summary let us emphasizes the critical importance of advocating for ending animal agriculture in the context of water conservation and sustainable resource management. It calls for a collective shift towards plant-based food systems, responsible water stewardship, and environmental sustainability to protect water resources, mitigate climate change, and create a more compassionate and sustainable future for all beings.

Chapter 17: Environmental Harmony: Bridging Environmental Justice and Animal Liberation

We have embarked on a transformative journey delving into the harmonious convergence of environmental justice and animal liberation. Amidst the calls for social equity, sustainable practices, and ethical treatment of animals, this chapter illuminates the interconnectedness of these movements, urging for a unified approach towards fostering a more compassionate and equitable world for all inhabitants.

Section 1: Embracing Environmental Justice

Embracing on the quest for environmental justice, the book champions the equitable dissemination of environmental benefits and burdens within society. Here, the narrative unpacks the disparities in environmental impacts, pollution burdens, and climate change vulnerabilities that disproportionately affect marginalized communities and fragile ecosystems. It emphasizes the imperative for inclusive and fair environmental policies that uphold the rights of all individuals and habitats.

Advocating for Animal Liberation

Unveiling the principles of animal liberation, this section passionately advocates for recognizing the inherent worth and rights of all sentient beings. It challenges conventional anthropocentric ideologies, advocates for ethical treatment of animals, and underscores the moral responsibilities intertwined with embracing compassion towards all creatures. The discourse navigates the ethical complexities, societal obligations, and moral imperatives associated with championing the cause of animal rights.

Interweaving Bonds of Justice and Compassion

Delving into the intricate tapestry of intersectionality, this section unearths the interconnected threads of environmental justice and animal liberation with broader social justice movements and sustainability endeavors. It explicates how addressing human, animal, and environmental welfare in unison lays the foundation for a more balanced, equitable, and empathetic world for all beings to thrive in. This section illuminates the path towards a holistic and inclusive approach to justice and compassion.

Advocacy Winds of Change

Navigating the realms of advocacy and activism in the pursuit of environmental justice and animal liberation, this section accentuates the pivotal role of grassroots movements, policy reform initiatives, and collective mobilization in steering societal transformation. It offers insights into effective strategies for raising consciousness, fostering diverse participation, and galvanizing concerted action towards reshaping systems and structures to amplify the voices of the marginalized and voiceless.

Forging a Sustainable World of Life

In the symphony of existence, this section underscores the necessity of weaving a sustainable tapestry for all beings to harmoniously coexist. It explores the transformative potential of integrating environmental justice principles, advocating for animal liberation, and instilling ethical considerations into the fabric of society. This final section envisions a world where environmental equanimity, social justice, and animal welfare converge to create a flourishing and balanced ecosystem for present and future generations.

Again in the closing notes of this chapter, we insist on the call to action, urging for a profound commitment to advancing environmental harmony through the nexus of environmental justice and animal liberation. It beckons for collaborative endeavors, empathetic deliberations, and inclusive practices to dismantle environmental injustices, amplify the voices of the voiceless, and illuminate the pathway towards a more interconnected, empathetic, and sustainable coexistence of humans, animals, and the environment.

Chapter 18: Animal Liberation in the Context of Sustainable Development Goals and Global Partnership

This last chapter explores transformative exploration of the Sustainable Development Goals (SDGs) crafted by the United Nations, heralding the imperative of global partnerships in driving progress towards these goals. This chapter delves into the symbiotic relationship between advocating for animal liberation and achieving sustainable development objectives on a global scale, highlighting the interconnectedness of social, economic, and environmental aspirations in shaping a more compassionate and sustainable world.

Aligning Animal Welfare with the Sustainable Development Goals

This section delves into aligning the cause of animal liberation with the 17 Sustainable Development Goals, underscoring the importance of incorporating animal welfare considerations into the broader framework of sustainable development. It explores how promoting humane treatment of animals can contribute to goals related to eradicating poverty, ensuring food security, combatting climate change, and fostering biodiversity conservation.

Global Partnerships for Animal Welfare

By examining the essential role of global partnerships in advancing animal welfare initiatives worldwide, this section illuminates the significance of collaboration among governments, international organizations, advocacy groups, and grassroots movements in advocating for animal rights and protection. It emphasizes the need for cross-sectoral cooperation and mutual support to drive positive change for animals on a global scale.

Monitoring Progress in Animal Welfare

Focusing on monitoring and evaluating progress in animal welfare standards, this section explores the development of indicators, data collection methodologies, and accountability frameworks to track advancements in animal liberation efforts. It underscores the importance of transparency, public engagement, and evidence-based decision-making in assessing the impact of policies and practices on animal well-being.

Addressing Challenges and Seizing Opportunities

Addressing the challenges and opportunities in advancing animal liberation within the context of the SDGs, this section navigates obstacles such as inadequate legal protections, animal exploitation industries, and cultural norms that perpetuate harm towards animals. It identifies opportunities for legislative reforms, public awareness campaigns, and ethical consumer choices to drive positive change and promote a more compassionate society.

Localizing Animal Welfare Initiatives

Highlighting the significance of localizing animal welfare initiatives at the community level, this section underscores the pivotal role of cities, regions, and grassroots organizations in implementing practices that prioritize animal well-being within their unique contexts. It discusses the importance of promoting humane education, fostering responsible pet ownership, and encouraging cruelty-free lifestyles to create a more animal-friendly world.

In concluding this author reinforces the call for integrating animal liberation within the broader framework of sustainable development, advocating for global partnerships that prioritize animal welfare as a crucial component of a sustainable and ethical future. It urges for collective action, cross-sector collaboration, and solidarity in championing the cause of animal rights as a fundamental pillar of sustainable development and global well-being.

Conclusion

As our exploration into the intricate realms of animal-human relationships and ethical considerations draws to a close, we find ourselves standing at the threshold of a profound revelation: the interconnectedness of all life forms and the imperative of compassion as the guiding light for a sustainable and harmonious future. Through the chapters that have unfolded, from delving into the shadows of history to unraveling the ethical progress towards animal liberation, from advocating for the moral value of sentient beings to dissecting the environmental toll of animal agriculture, we have traversed a rich tapestry of insights, challenges, and transformation.

The shadows of history have cast a stark light on the complex dynamics that have shaped our interactions with animals through the annals of time. From companionship to exploitation, from reverence to disregard, our journey alongside our fellow sentient beings has been one marked by evolution, reflection, and the call to reassess our relationship with the natural world that sustains us. The urgency of change rings clear through the clarion call for liberation championed by organizations like PETA, urging us to confront societal norms, traditions, and practices that perpetuate cruelty and injustice towards animals.

As we journey through the realms of ethical progress and environmental consciousness, we are confronted with profound truths about our interconnectedness with all living beings and the delicate balance that sustains life on Earth. The moral value of sentient beings beckons us to extend empathy, care, and respect to all creatures, transcending species boundaries to embrace a compassionate perspective rooted in kindness, understanding, and ethical responsibility. From the gentle soulfulness of dogs and cats to the stoic grace of cows, our acknowledgment of sentience across species opens the door to a paradigm shift from exploitation to respect, inviting us to forge new pathways of interaction founded on reverence and ethical stewardship.

The environmental toll of animal agriculture looms large on the horizon, casting a shadow of greenhouse gas emissions, climate change impacts, habitat destruction, and biodiversity loss that reverberates through the delicate web of life. Documentaries like "Seaspiracy" and "Cowspiracy" serve as stark reminders of the hidden costs of our dietary choices, prompting a critical examination of the linkages between animal agriculture and environmental degradation. The case for a ban on animal agriculture emerges as a compelling imperative grounded in ethical and environmental considerations, while the embrace of veganism and plant-based diets emerges as a tangible path towards reducing ecological footprints and combating environmental degradation.

In the dawning light of hope and transformation, we see a paradigm shift towards animal liberation and plant-based living as a strategy for environmental sustainability and ethical evolution. The linkage between animal agriculture and environmental damage becomes undeniably clear, prompting a collective call to action towards a compassionate future where healing our planet is not just a goal, but a shared responsibility. Through collective action, conscious choices, and a steadfast commitment to compassion, we pave the path towards a future where all beings - human, animal, and environmental

- coexist in harmony, respect, and reverence for the intricate web of life that binds us all.

As we conclude this journey through the chapters of history, ethics, advocacy, and transformation, we stand at the precipice of a compassionate future beckoning us to take the next step towards healing our planet through collective action. The path to a compassionate future is not just a destination but a continuous journey of introspection, growth, and solidarity with all sentient beings. It is a call to arms to rise above the shadows of the past, to embrace the urgency of change, and to forge a new legacy of hope, transformation, and collective action in service of a world where compassion reigns supreme, and all beings thrive in unity, respect, and interconnectedness.